DUBLIN
CAROL

DUBLIN CAROL

A PLAY

CONOR McPHERSON

THEATRE COMMUNICATIONS GROUP

Dublin Carol is published by Theatre Communications Group, Inc.,
355 Lexington Ave., New York, NY 10017–6603.

Dublin Carol is published in arrangement with
Nick Hern Books Limited, The Glasshouse, 49a, Goldhawk Road,
Shepherd's Bush, London, England W12 8QP.

This publication is made possible in part with public funds from
the New York State Council on the Arts, a State Agency.

TCG books are exclusively distributed to the book trade by Consortium
Book Sales and Distribution, 1045 Westgate Dr., St. Paul, MN 55114.

LIBRARY OF CONGRESS CATALOGING-IN-PUBLICATION DATA
McPherson, Conor, 1971–
Dublin carol / by Conor McPherson.— 1st ed.
p. cm.
ISBN 1-55936-185-9 (alk. paper)
1. Fathers and daughters—Drama. 2. Dublin (Ireland)—Drama.
3. Divorced men—Drama. 4. Christmas—Drama.
I. Title.
PR6063.C73 D8   2000
822'.914—dc21   00-037757

Book design and typography by Lisa Govan
Cover design by Lisa Govan
Cover photograph by the author

First edition November 2000

DUBLIN
CAROL

For Ríonach

and for my family

PRODUCTION HISTORY

Dublin Carol premiered at London's Royal Court Theatre on February 22, 2000. The director was Ian Rickson, with set and costume design by Rae Smith, lighting design by Paule Constable, sound design by Paul Arditti and original music by Stephen Warbeck. The cast was as follows:

JOHN	Brian Cox
MARK	Andrew Scott
MARY	Bronagh Gallagher

Dublin Carol opened at Dublin's Gate Theatre on October 3, 2000. The director was Robin Leserve, with set and costume design by Liz Ascroft and lighting design by Mick Hughes. The cast was as follows:

JOHN	John Cavanagh
MARK	Sean McDonagh
MARY	Donna Dent

CHARACTERS

JOHN, late fifties
MARK, early twenties
MARY, thirties

PLACE

The play is set over one day, 24 December:

PART ONE, late morning
PART TWO, early afternoon
PART THREE, late afternoon

The action takes place in an office on the Northside of Dublin, around Fairview or the North Strand Road.

N O T E: any laughter denoted between the characters need not be literal. Tiny breaths or smiles may suffice and it's up to the actors to find their own rhythm and pitch in rehearsal.

PART
ONE

✠

An office. Dublin. The present.

The office is furnished with old wooden desks, carpet, comfortable chairs, filing cabinets, tasteful paintings, elaborate lamps. But all a bit old and musty. In one corner is a sink with cups, teapot, kettle, etc. There is an electric fire. There are terribly scrawny Christmas decorations. A few fairy lights. A foot-high plastic Christmas tree on one of the desks. A little Advent calendar with just a few doors left to open.

Mark, a young man of about twenty comes in. He wears a black suit and an overcoat. He looks a bit wet. He stands in the office for a few moments by himself, as though waiting to be told what to do.

Then John, fifties, comes in. He also wears a black suit and overcoat. He's not quite as wet as Mark.

JOHN

Sorry. I had to make a call. Get your wet gear off, Mark, yeah?

MARK

Yeah.

JOHN

I'll put the kettle on.

(John fills the kettle. Mark takes his coat off and looks for somewhere to put it. He drapes it over a chair and stands with his hands in his pockets.)

Plug in that old fire there.

(Mark goes down beside a desk and plugs the fire in.)

You did very well.

MARK

Really?

JOHN

Oh yeah.

(John takes off his coat and takes a hanger from a hook on the door. He hangs his coat up. He takes a towel from beside the sink and tosses it to Mark. Mark rubs his hair.)

Give your head a rub.

MARK

Thanks Mr. Plunkett.

JOHN

Sit down there.

(Mark sits on a chair. John stays near the sink and farts around with the tea. He takes a small bottle of whiskey from a drawer and pours some into a cup.)

I'm not gonna offer you any of this, son. Your ma'd kill me. I'm old. I'll die if I don't drink this.

MARK

(Laughs) That's alright.

JOHN

I have to have a sup of this.

(Pause.)

You can have a cup of tea in a minute. *(Short pause)* When the kettle boils up. You know what I mean?

(They laugh.)

Yeah . . . There's an old pub there across the road, you know? The Strand.

MARK

Yeah I was in there.

JOHN

Yeah?

MARK

Yeah I was in there last night. After work. My girlfriend came down and met me there.

JOHN

Yeah?

MARK

Yeah. She knew it.

JOHN

Yeah?

MARK

Yeah. She knew it from before. She used to work down there in the stationery place.

JOHN

Oh right. Where's she from?

MARK

Marino.

JOHN

Ah well, then, you know?

MARK

Yeah.

JOHN

Up the road.

MARK

Yeah.

JOHN

She's only down the road. A lot of people would know it. Your man does give the regulars a Christmas drink and all this.

MARK

Yeah. It was fairly busy. A lot of people going home from work.

JOHN

Ah yeah, they do a, they used to always do a nice lunch, and you'd get all the people going in there for their nosh. You used to see a lot of priests going in. And that's . . . did you ever hear that, that's a sign the food is good, you know?

(They laugh.)

Because they know what side their bread is buttered on. That's a little hint for you there now. The old girlfriend, ha? Does she still work up there?

MARK

No she's an air hostess.

JOHN

Oh ho!

(Mark laughs.)

Very, "How's it fuckin' goin' . . ."

MARK

(Slightly embarrassed) Yep.

JOHN

The uniform.

MARK

Yep.

JOHN

Did you meet her on a plane?

MARK

Nah. Met her at a party.

JOHN

With the uniform and all.

MARK

(Laughs, thinks) I don't like the uniform.

JOHN

Why?

MARK

I don't know. It makes her legs look fat.

JOHN

Ah now here. Where are you going with that kind of talk?
Bloody air hostess, man.

MARK

Well you're going a bit mad about it.

(They laugh.)

JOHN

I know. What's her name?

MARK

Kim.

JOHN

Kim?

MARK

Yeah.

JOHN

That's eh, that's not an Irish name.

MARK

Mmm. I don't know what it is.

JOHN

Is it short for something?

MARK

I don't know.

JOHN

Kipling or . . . Nn. What's she like?

MARK

Em. She's sort of dark. Like her skin is kind of dark.

JOHN

What, sort of tanned or kind of yellowy?

MARK

(Laughs) Yeah kind of.

JOHN

Was she on her holidays?

MARK

No. She just is.

JOHN

Janey Mack. There's people'd love that, you know?

MARK

Yeah.

JOHN

Are you going out long?

MARK

Going out a year and three months.

JOHN

Oh my God. This is the big one, ha?

MARK

You never know.

JOHN

If it's there, it's there, you know? But ah . . . *(Thinks better of what he is going to say)* . . . you know? How old are you, son?

MARK

Twenty.

JOHN

Jesus. Twenty. God. I don't know. Grasp the nettle. *(Short pause)* But you obviously don't have any trouble there. In that department.

MARK

(Good-naturedly) Give me a break, will you?

JOHN

I'm sorry. Hangover. Has me chatty. You did very well today, do you know that?

MARK

Did I really?

JOHN

Oh yeah. Very good. You're a natural.

(Mark grimaces slightly as if to say, "This better not be my calling.")

MARK

Do you not find it kind of horrible, though?

JOHN

Ah that person was young, Mark. I'm telling you, it's not usually like that. People get older, they're naturally kind of ready for it, you know? And everybody knows that. And it's all a few quid for the priest and soup and sandwiches in the Addison Lodge. You know? It's different with old people. You get used to it. You were very good. Helping that girl.

MARK

(Hoping John agrees) She couldn't drive.

JOHN

(Matter-of-factly) No. *(Sly pause)* What do you reckon? Was she a bit on the side.

MARK

(Catching on) Maybe an old girlfriend or something, alright.

JOHN

He was a drug addict, you know?

MARK

Oh really, yeah?

JOHN

See the amount of fucking young ones? I'd say he was a right little cunt, d'you ever get that feeling? Three and four timing them left right and center. Did you not see his little missus. Shooting daggers all round the grave?

MARK

Really?

JOHN

It was a mess! *(Short pause)* Do you think I'm very callous, Mark, yeah?

MARK

No.

JOHN

I often think I must be. But with Noel out sick, and me having to run things a little bit. I've been having a . . . *(Although almost certain of something)* Are you supposed to just fucking . . .

MARK

Yeah . . . ?

JOHN

No I'm just *(As though this is what he's been wondering about)* you'd think this kettle would never boil. I don't drink loads of tea. It's a thing with it that people go mad to put the kettle on. I know I'm after putting it on now, but we're wet and so on. But people do be falling all over themselves to be giving you tea all the time.

(Distant church bells ring out.)

Do you go to mass?

MARK

No.

JOHN

The same as meself. Why d'you not go?

MARK

I don't know. It's hard to eh . . . *(Almost unexpectedly deflates)* Psss. I don't know. I just don't go I suppose.

JOHN

Yeah . . . I haven't gone in years either, you know? Although I feel like I do because there's always mass going on at the funeral. Outside the porch, or sitting in the car like we were today. Go in at the end. Help the poor lads who want to carry the coffin and all this. Nobody carried it today. But you'll get it where they want to. But it should feel like it's a big part of my life because you do always be in churches all the time.

MARK

Well it is, isn't it? Big part of your life. You're more . . . than most people, you know?

JOHN

(Slightly vainly, as though they should get the details of his life correct) I'm around it. You know?

MARK

Yeah . . .

JOHN

Are you a Christmas man?

MARK

Yeah, I suppose I am. I like Christmas.

JOHN

Get the little lady a present and so on.

MARK

Well I suppose you have to, don't you? You know?

JOHN

Ah you have to. Get her a nice jumper or something.

(They laugh.)

MARK

Get her a nice anorak.

JOHN

Oh she'll be delighted. Nice pair of socks in the pockets. Little surprise, you know?

(They laugh.)

MARK

God. Imagine.

JOHN

Oh there's lads and they do things like that. Buying the wives cutlery and toasters and all sorts of shite. But then again, a lot of it is shite. You know?

(They laugh.)

Fucking hairdriers.

(They laugh.)

You know in the pictures you never see a baldy Indian. In the cowboys and Indians.

MARK

(Thinks) Yeah.

JOHN

That's you don't wash your hair. You never see a bald knacker. You see the itinerants. They let the natural oils do the business. There's not all hairdriers in the caravans and all this.

MARK

Do you have to get many presents?

JOHN

Ah sure not anymore. A boy over in England there, and, you know . . . Jesus I never made you any fucking tea.

(John goes to make tea.)

We can't be having that.

MARK

No, it's fine. I have to go.

JOHN

We never did the Advent calendar. You do it.

(Mark goes to the Advent calendar and opens a little door on it. John makes tea for Mark.)

What is it?

MARK

Ahm. It's little angels, like in a choir.

JOHN

A feast of heavenly angels, is it? No it's a host of heavenly angels. "A feast." I'm losing the marbles entirely at this stage. Have you gone in to see your Uncle Noel?

MARK

Not yet, no, I haven't. I should go really.

JOHN

Yeah. Ah he's not very well, you know?

MARK

Yeah?

JOHN

Yeah. *(Actively reassuring)* He'll get better. But just it's not great, in the hospital for Christmas, you know?

MARK

Mmm.

JOHN

But the nurses are great and all that. They help you, you know?

MARK

Yeah.

JOHN

Poor fella. I went in last night. And it was after visiting hours, because of the removal. There was no one kind of in there. Not even the full lights on and all this. And I think whatever they do to try and have people home at Christmas, there was only one other fella there in the ward. Some auldfella. And he was asleep. And Noelly was there with the telly on, only low, watching some terrible shite altogether. And I was sitting

there with him, and he was very tired from all the tests and all
this they were doing on him. And it just felt like I should be
trying to get him out. Like a jailbreak or something.

(They smile.)

It was all kind of blue, and just the light coming off the telly
(Ominously) on the shiny floor. Aw, it's a different world.
You're very helpless. Like the doctors say it's all looking good.
But ah . . . Do you know what it was. It was kind of embar-
rassing. Having to ask if you can do your toilet and all. He
had a bit of an upset stomach. From whatever tablets they
give him. And instead of asking the nurse for a bit of something, he was lying there and kind of bearing up, you know?

(They laugh.)

And I said, ah, here, I'll lash out to the nurse. Nurse sitting
out there on her own at the station. And I go, "Your man in
here is feeling a bit yucky, you know?" And she was grand,
like. No problem. She gave him this bit of medicine, there,
the sad eyes looking up at her. *(Laughs)* It's terrible, isn't it.
Grown-up man. Although. Maybe we all like a bit of pam-
pering. What do you think?

MARK

(Laughs) We might. Yeah.

JOHN

Mmm. He was great for me. I was very very messy at one
time, you know? And he gave me a start here. Got me back
into a normal . . . He's a good man. But he will, he'll get out,
and he'll be back here. Might give you a bit of a better start
here if you want. More permanent. He'll need people.

MARK

Yeah. Well I think I'm gonna try to go to college next year.

JOHN

Oh very good!

MARK

Yeah.

JOHN

Yeah. *(Beat)* Your mam was saying you were kind of kicking around a bit. No offense.

MARK

No, she's right, you're right. I have been, you know? Been out of school for three years now. And whatever I've been doing. I haven't eh you know.

JOHN

You see, you haven't settled in anywhere.

MARK

Yeah.

JOHN

Well, Jesus, don't worry about it yet, you're only twenty years of age. It's not like you've killed somebody!

(They laugh.)

You'll find your niche. This was mine.

MARK

Is it not anymore?

JOHN

Aw no, it is, it has been, I mean. When I found it. And if college isn't starting until next September or whenever it is, you could do a lot worse than this.

MARK

Mmm.

JOHN

It can be sad. But there is a dignity to it. *(Short pause)* Because you're trying to find the dignity. You're trying to afford people a bit of respect in their last little bit with their family and the people around them. Funeral is for the people left behind. That's what it's for. It's not for the dead person. I don't think. Mmm. When I go though—very small.

MARK

Yeah?

JOHN

Keeping it all very quiet.

MARK

(With good-humored amusement) Yeah?

JOHN

Spare people the old hassle.

MARK

But what if people want to pay their respect to you?

JOHN

Ah respect is no use to you when you're gone. If you don't earn it while you're alive, don't be looking for it just because you've happened to die. I never really did any great things. In fact, I've done many things which, to tell you the truth, I'm very very ashamed of. And if you've let people down, don't be wanting them to be all crowding around talking about what a brilliant fella you were, at your funeral, you know? *(With a certain resigned emphatic quality)* I've seen enough funerals where people have been genuinely heartbroken for me to expect for people to be, you know, mourning me and all this. I just want to slip away, you know? Very quiet. Under cover of darkness.

(They give a little laugh.)

The great escape.

MARK

Yeah. Very morbid.

(They laugh.)

JOHN

Well. It fucking is. You know?

(They laugh.)

Good Jaysus, these decorations are scaldy.

MARK

(Laughs) They're not the best, alright.

JOHN

I don't know. What do we want? Flashing . . . fairy lights . . . But of course you know, we have to be a bit cool because we have so many people in here recently bereaved. We can't have flashing lights and and Ding Dong Merrily on High and, *(With physicality)* "Ah! How's it going?" You know?

(Mark spits out his tea laughing.)

Ah now here. Tea going everywhere and everything now. God, you get those fellas crooning all bloody Christmas. It's a real slippers and pipe job. In the rocking chair. Do you ever see that?

MARK

(A little laugh) Yeah.

JOHN

Jays, it was great. I used to love all that, you know? The bloody lengths I used to go to. I was worse than the kids. Hiding presents all over the place. Leaving out cake and a drink for Santy. I spent an hour one Christmas eve telling them Santy didn't like sherry. He liked Macardle's.

(They laugh.)

Because it was for me, you know? *(Pause)* Tch. Jaysus. You know?

(Pause.)

Long time ago now, you know?

(Silence. Mark seems to get ready to go.)

MARK

I better eh . . .

JOHN

(As though stopping him) D'you want a biscuit, here, did you have your breakfast?

MARK

I'm grand, I don't really ever eat breakfast.

JOHN

What?

MARK

I have to go anyway. I have to do some stuff.

JOHN

(Almost desperately opening a packet of biscuits, offering them to Mark) Well, you know, you have to . . . you can't be . . . Like I don't care what you do normally. But you're standing out in the cold now. You have to have a bit of fuel in you. Keep you going you know, on your feet all day. In all weathers. Noelly got me in the habit. I used to be like you. I'd nearly be puking if someone put a load of food in front of me in the morning. God, I didn't know how people could do it.

(Mark finally has a biscuit and stays a little longer. John's slight hysteria subsides and he relaxes, becoming direct with Mark.)

At the same time, I was at a time, in my life, where I was very dependent on drink. D'you understand me?

MARK

(Affirmative) Mmm-hmm.

JOHN

Not that I don't drink now. I still drink. You know? But not in the way that I used to. And the way I was then, Jaysus you'd wake up in the morning and you'd still be very pissed. But horrible. I'm telling you this because this is the story of how I met your Uncle Noel, yeah?

MARK

Yeah, yeah.

JOHN

You'd want to die. All you could do, this'd be the routine, was hang on till opening time, in you'd go. One or two lads in the same predicament. The big red faces, and the big swollen fuckin' heads. God the first one or two pints'd knock the fuckin' head off you, but then one or two more, and you'd be feeling a bit better, head home or wherever you call home, you'd probably be able to lie down and get a bit of kip then. Up you'd get, six or seven and off out into the night. Winter nights and summer nights. Winter nights the steam coming off everybody's wet coats. And the stink of all those dirty bastards leaning into you and snoring in the bar. Summer nights. God, it's amazing what the weather does, nothing's as bad, is it? You'd actually be making the effort. Having a shave and every fucking thing. Clean shirt. Down on the road, waiting on the bus in the summer breeze. Good God. *(Short pause)*

Now I wasn't always like that and I haven't been like that since. But this is because of, thanks to Noelly. Bloody fucking . . . you know, got me. Sorted me out. Got talking to him in the pub across the road. You know what he's like. All . . . *(Raises himself up)* You know, the bearing. You know?

(They smile.)

MARK

Yeah.

JOHN

He was one of them people. Still is. Always sat there on his own, reading the paper. Very much his own man, and keeping himself to himself. But what you'd notice about him was that he seemed to know everybody. They'd all be saying hello to him, he'd be very much on for a quick chat, crack a joke or whatever. But then back to himself. Very much at peace. And one time I asked someone, you know, who is your man? What does he do? An' when they said, "Undertaker," you know. It was like. "Oh right." That makes sense. I can see that. And one time, whatever happened, I was there and there wasn't very many people there and I was with someone who knew him. This was very civilized drinking. That's why that was always a great pub. The staff were very good. Very discreet. Never any messing. I've been in some terrible fucking places. Filthy dirty places. Big rows all the time and all. Fucking barman would have a mattress down behind the bar, fucking be living there and every fucking thing, you know? I mean, Jesus. But across the road there, used to be called Hannigan's then. Very good. And whatever happened this time, there were very few people there and Noel came in and sat up at the bar like everyone else and he was chatting away, very dry wit. Had us all in stitches. And he bought me a drink and I got chatting to him on his own. He had a great, and he still has it, a great listening quality, you have it as well.

(Mark smiles a little self-consciously.)

And I was chatting away, this and that and I began to tell him a bit about myself. Not in any fucking-stupid-pisshead-very-sorry-for-myself way or anything, anything, like that. But I explained that I was in a bit of a mess. I had gotten myself into a terrible mess. This is many years ago. And I had gone to the stage where I was down to the very last bit of my savings, and I was out of work because I'd basically, no two ways about it, I'd hit the bottle goodo. And I was in and out of my house and I was going to end up on the, the, fucking skids, you know? Be a tramp, you know?

(John is slightly distressed for a second. Just a glimpse of something, a flash in the face.)

It was an extremely bad situation. *(Short pause)* Now to be fair, I wasn't looking for anything off him. Sure you wouldn't expect for someone to do what he did. I was just basically telling him the truth. And I was generally getting things off my chest. And right there, he says come on back and have a bite and this. Went back, came in here, sat down like where you are and he offers me a job.

You know. Give me a start. And eh . . . God I didn't want to let him down. But your pride kicks in as well. I didn't want to be a charity case on anybody's back. But he sensed that too, you know? And he was able to phrase it properly, more like he needed me more than I needed him, and it was simply a fortuitous thing that had happened—us meeting up. And there was a spare room and all this.

I was so tired. Not just from it being the nighttime and everything. But in general. Up he goes and lights a fire in the room. Gives me a pair of pajamas. What was I like?

(They smile.)

I was like something out of Peter Pan and Wendy or something. All I needed now was a little Teddy bear.

(They laugh.)

Jesus. But fair dues. What got me on to this? Oh yes! Breakfast!

(They laugh.)

He gets me up in the morning. God. A huge big fry. Rashers and eggs and everything. Pots of tea. Loads of toast. And it got me in the habit. Which is the point I was making.
   Mmm.

MARK

What was the job?

JOHN

Same as you today. Carrying wreaths. Lifting out the coffin. And excuse the pun, but generally looking grave. Looking grave and somber. I'm not a mortician, now, like Noel. There were two other men that were here then. Old Paddy McDermott and Andy Stafford. They're gone now, retired and everything . . . Quiet fellas, you know? And you couldn't bring the subject up . . . But, you see, Noelly would take us all over for a few pints a couple of nights a week. It was like, fucking, like a supervised drink. These were older fellas now. Big lads. Low gruff . . . *(Hunches over)* . . . voices. And Noelly would buy a few rounds, you know. And I often wondered if, the two boys were . . . if they'd got these jobs in the same way, you know, that I did. Like your Uncle Noel was some . . . He's a very good man, you know?

MARK

Mmm.

JOHN

The more I think about them now. Years on from them. I always remember them as very battered men. They were like they'd had the shit kicked out of them, you know?

(Mark is genuinely interested in all of this. His prospects lie ahead of him, and what the world has in store.)

I think Andy had even been in prison for something. But you'd never ask. But they weren't know-alls like you get in so many pubs in Dublin. God, there's some terrible fucking eejits. The fellas who fucked your ma and forgave your da for letting them. You know?

(Mark nearly loses his tea again.)

Did you never hear that one? Jesus there's some awful men. I'm a Dublin man. Sometimes I wish maybe if I'd lived out in the country, what the hell would I've been like. Probably the same. Bullshit artist.

(They smile.)

But eh . . . he'd take us over for a pint. But we did see some awful stuff at the same time. Suicides and a woman been killed one time, you know?

MARK

What's the worst thing you've seen?

JOHN

Baby born down a toilet.

MARK

What?!

JOHN

Ah this fucking thing, young girl got pregnant from some fella, some uncle or someone. Course she had no idea what was going on. One because she was fourteen and two because a lot of these people are very stupid and nobody thought there was anything wrong with her. Middle of the night then, she wakes up. In labor. On to the jacks for a few hours. She tried to flush it away but it blocked up the plumbing. I didn't see it down the toilet. I only saw it after.

But ahm . . . And this is the other side of it. I was once over picking up a job in Terenure. This house, wasn't much to look at outside. But inside it was all beautiful. Set back from the road. All the walls knocked in on the inside.

MARK

Open plan.

JOHN

Yes. And big bright airy windows. Very peaceful with the wind going through the leaves out there in the back. And a big long wooden table when we arrived. And a bottle of the hard stuff and a couple of glasses there for us—this was a suicide and the guards had been, and it looked all fairly cut and dry. Little old man up in the bed. Tiny wasted away. Sleeping pills and booze there beside the bed. Note and all this. He was, or had been, sick from cancer. And took his own life. Very calm there. Very peaceful. Me and Andy sort of looked down at him in the bed, but we didn't move him for a while. We just sort of went and sat at the big table and stole a nip of the scotch or whatever it was was there. Very relaxed or something. All around were plants and statues of what do you call it? Buddha. *(Pause)* Mmm. Paddy. Andy. Broken noses and generally battered by life. But never the complaint. Never the fucking moaning Minnie. Unlike my good self. Eejit boy. That's the superhero I'd be. "We need to have this fucked-up immediately! Quick! Get Eejit Boy!" Who'd you be?

MARK

Horny Man.

(They burst out laughing.)

JOHN

The man with the horn, ha?

MARK

Yeah.

(They are quiet for a moment.)

JOHN

You might as well be on your way. Come and get your money later.

MARK

Alright.

JOHN

Come in in the afternoon.

MARK

Okay.

JOHN

Good man and well done.

(Mark leaves.

John puts the cups on the sink. He goes and puts his own coat on, an anorak. He takes the bottle of whiskey and puts the top on it. He stretches. He unplugs the fire. He coughs.)

(Absentmindedly as he leaves) "Buddha."

(The lights fade.)

PART
TWO

�֤

Mary comes into the office. She is in her thirties and seems very tired. She looks around a little bit. Then she sits.

John comes into the office. He carries a bag from the off licence.

JOHN

I'm sorry. I had to run across the road.

(He takes a bottle of whiskey from the bag and opens it. He is dying to get a drink into him.)

MARY

You still . . .

JOHN

Oh nowhere near! This is shocking news, Mary. And I had to get a few bits for the Christmas. Will you have a drink?

MARY

It's a bit early.

JOHN

Ah Jaysus, shocking news though. For me.

MARY

Just give me a little bit.

JOHN

Yes. I'm glad. Not drinking on my own.

(John gives them both a drink of neat whiskey in old mugs. John shoots his back in one, his eyes nearly coming out on stalks. He

immediately pours himself another. Mary takes a sip from hers.
It's too strong for her.)

MARY

Can I have a drop of water?

JOHN

Oh yes, of course.

(He takes her drink over to the sink and pours some water in.)

We're really closed but I have to give a youngfella his wages
later. So handier here.

MARY

That's fine.

JOHN

This is terrible news. I'll have to sort out going in.

MARY

Oh you have to . . . ?

JOHN

Well I should I think. I think I should.

MARY

Of course you should! What are you talking about?

JOHN

I'm just saying I have to go in.

MARY

Of course you have to.

JOHN

What's wrong?

MARY

Just you make it like such a chore. For you.

JOHN

No. Just I've been in and out seeing Noel, the man who runs this business. And it's just. Going to the hospital. I don't know. I didn't mean anything.

MARY

(Softens a little) Come with me today.

JOHN

What time are you going in at?

MARY

I could pick you up at five or something. *(Pause)* Okay?

JOHN

(Awkward, guarded) Is Paul gonna come home?

MARY

He's coming on Monday.

JOHN

How is he, alright, yeah?

MARY

The same as me, just can't believe it.

JOHN

But in general.

MARY

He fixes motorbikes, with this friend of his.

JOHN

English fella.

MARY

Yeah.

JOHN

What, like you go over?

MARY

I just been twice. I was there in the summer.

JOHN

But he's alright.

MARY

Yeah he's . . . He's the same as he was. Drifts along. He's getting like you though, more and more.

JOHN

Yeah? God.

*(A slightly awkward moment passes between them which Mary
breaks, just for something to say.)*

MARY

I don't know if I could live there.

JOHN

Yeah?

MARY

(Direct, almost without expression) It's like Coronation Street.
That's what it's like. That's what it looks like.

JOHN

Yeah?

MARY

The little streets. All little terraced houses and all. Up and
down these hills. When I was there. Every day it was you go
around the corner and either get a pizza or an Indian or a
Chinese.

JOHN

Out of the take-away.

MARY

(Regaining expression and lucidity) Yeah. Yeah. Just do that all the time. His friend Craig comes around and they stand in this little back garden drinking beer and tinkering around with motorbikes. I used to go and sit in this graveyard.

JOHN

How is he getting like me?

MARY

The way he says things and nods. The way he stands in the pub and things like that.

JOHN

And what do yous say? About me and all that?

MARY

He doesn't . . . He doesn't say anything. About you.

(John exhales deeply.)

You look much older.

JOHN

Yeah?

(Mary nods.)

I am older, you know? D'you want another drink?

MARY

No.

(John pours himself one.)

JOHN

Little smartener.

MARY

Yeah. *(Again softens a little, brings John in)* He has this horrible girlfriend.

39

JOHN

Yeah?

MARY

Yeah well she's not really anymore. But she doesn't leave him alone. She's a little scrawny thing. Her hair is in bits. And she has terrible acne because she only eats pub grub and chocolate. She's like a little monkey. She gets pissed and comes 'round to his house. It was very funny. She came around one day and we had to lie down in the living room near the wall so she couldn't see us. Me and Paul and Craig. God, it was hard not make any noise, I was bursting out laughing. I thought I was going to wet myself. She was there for ages. One of the neighbors even came out and asked her what was wrong with her. God it was awful. She's a bit mad, like, I think.

JOHN

Tch.

(They look at each other.)

MARY

She caught us in one night. It was so hot we had the front door open. Because there's no hall, just the front room where we were sitting. In she walks. It was awful. She plonked herself down and started just talking. It was so weird. She wouldn't go. I just went up to bed. But she was there in the morning. She only went when me and Paul pretended to go out.

JOHN

(A little laugh) Mmm.

(Pause.)

MARY

Mmm.

JOHN

How are you doing? I'm sorry, this is very hard.

MARY

Yeah, I'm . . . I'm working in Dunnes. In Stephen's Green.

JOHN

Oh right. Okay.

MARY

It's alright, you know. It's okay.

JOHN

Well that's alright, isn't it?

MARY

(Looks around, no pause) I'll have to do all this . . . funeral . . .

(Silence.)

JOHN

What else are you doing?

MARY

I don't know. Sometimes I drive down the country. Wonder what the fuck I'm doing there and come back.

JOHN

You remember down in Limerick. Where we used to go.

MARY

Yeah. When Paul lost his shoes.

JOHN

Oh God yeah. Jesus. The ructions.

MARY

Mmm.

JOHN

We had some great times down there. You might have been
too young.

MARY

No I remember. I remember Paul losing his shoes. I remember standing in the middle of a load of nettles one time.
Couldn't go anywhere without being stung. Just standing
there in this little sleeveless dress I loved. Getting stung to
bits. You came in through the nettles and lifted me out.

JOHN

Yeah.

MARY

I remember one night. We were all in the house and you hadn't
come home. Auntie Rita wanted Mam to ring the guards. Or
ring the hospitals to see what had happened. But Mam knew
you'd come back.

JOHN

I was gone to the pictures.

MARY

What?!

JOHN

I mean first.

MARY

Yeah, not all night.

JOHN

Yeah I went to the pub.

MARY

Oh, Duh . . .

JOHN

Yeah well that's where I was.

MARY

Course you were.

JOHN

I used to get caught down the country. Up home they kick
you out at eleven. But you'd be chancing a quick one like that,
those boys'll (i.e., barmen in the country) serve you till two
o'clock in the morning. So you'd think you were catching
them for a quick one after the pictures. But the door'd be
locked and it was just getting going.

MARY

Do you know how many years it is, since I've seen you?

JOHN

I don't know.

MARY

That day I met you on Henry Street and we went for a cup
of coffee.

JOHN

Oh yeah? . . .

MARY

That's ten years ago.

JOHN

Okay.

MARY

And you're still, you're still making bloody excuses about a
night in Limerick, what twenty-five years ago. I just, I don't
believe it.

JOHN

Well, I'm telling you.

MARY

I know. But. Here I am. I don't know what to call you. Our lives are . . .

JOHN

It happens a lot.

MARY

(Marveling at him) But you're still, here making excuses.

JOHN

But what do you want me to say?

MARY

I don't know. But it's like you're treating me like a fool. "I'd get caught . . . A quick one after the pictures . . ." If you even went to the pictures. When Mam was in hospital having Paul, I remember Auntie Rita came to stay. You slept in with me. And you had a bottle of something up in the wardrobe. I woke up and you were sitting down against the radiator.

JOHN

I couldn't sleep.

MARY

See again, there's an excuse.

JOHN

Of course there's an excuse. You think I'd deliberately want to hurt you? I wish it was different. But that's what I needed to do.

MARY

Yeah but do you not . . . *(The rest is unspeakable)*

(Silence. John explodes.)

JOHN

What do you want me to say about it? I'm not going to just say, "I'm sorry"—because of the fucking enormity of all the fucking things I did. It's not enough. Jesus. I know. I know. I think about everybody. You're telling me Helen is going to die?! Where am I supposed to be? I remember her years ago. Jesus, how can I go and look at that? Should I, even?

MARY

You're her husband.

JOHN

I'm not her fucking husband! What kind of fucking husband am I? That's all gone.

MARY

It'd mean a lot to her.

(Pause.)

JOHN

She wants me to go?

(Mary nods. John closes his eyes and hangs his head.)

Tch.

(He makes a long hissing sigh.)

What goes through people's minds? *(Short pause)* Is she in a state, like?

MARY

No she's exhausted just. You'd want to see her if it was you.

JOHN

No I wouldn't. I'd want it all over quick as possible.

MARY

No I don't believe that.

JOHN

(Tone of, "That's your opinion") Well.

MARY

I'd want to see you.

(Pause.)

JOHN

Why?

(Pause.)

MARY

Because I love you.

(Long pause.)

JOHN

Why do you love me?

MARY

I can't help it. I always think about you. And I . . . *(Matter-of-factly)* I hate you too.

JOHN

I think about you as well, you know? Don't do this.

(Pause.)

MARY

I had this boyfriend. He wasn't my boyfriend. I don't know what I was thinking. He was, this friend of mine at work, he was her brother. He was a big . . . they're from Kildare. He was a big culchie, teacher. Primary schoolteacher. I met him when we were out one night. There's this place, Major Tom's. I was. I just wanted something to happen. He was there. A big shiny red face. I didn't . . . I wasn't serious about him. I saw him a few times. Drinking stupid cocktails around those places up there around the center. And I just came up the steps with him one night, into the street. And whatever it was, the way the buildings looked, it took me back in time. And I felt that, you . . . I felt that you were with me. And this guy Ger, he was always pissed. He wanted me to go back to his house with him. And I know this is weird, but it was like he was, compared to you, even as a messer, compared to you, he was such a fucking amateur.

(They give a little laugh.)

Do you know? That even in the morning all he'd complain about would be his hangover and how he had copybooks to correct. Where you'd be looking for money to hit the bottle . . .

JOHN

Which is terrible . . .

(They are smiling a little, John shaking his head.)

For who I was and who you were and what I should have been looking for money for.

MARY

Sometimes I smell you. Everything comes back.

JOHN

I know.

MARY

I can smell it now.

JOHN

It's Brut.

(Pause.)

MARY

Do you still see . . . Carol? . . .

47

JOHN

Oh, no. I don't even want to talk about it.

MARY

I know she didn't take you away. I know she looked after you.

JOHN

She kept me going. She liked me too much. Warts and all. Horrible characteristics and everything. That was the problem. Would've watched me kill myself if that was what I wanted.

MARY

I remember the weekend you left.

JOHN

Don't . . .

MARY

It was a Friday, you came to collect me from school. And it was usually Mam and I came out and whatever was going on, it was you instead of her. And I remember you could hardly stand without swaying. You were hanging on to the railings and we went to get the bus. And the smell of drink off you.

JOHN

I know.

MARY

And you didn't know what the hell you were doing, and we went and got the bus on the wrong side of the road.

JOHN

This is all a long time ago.

MARY

And we went into town! And you couldn't talk properly or anything.

48

JOHN

I know.

MARY

Jesus. Neither of us knew where the hell we were. I was only seven. And you must've been drinking for days.

JOHN

I know.

MARY

And you took me into a pub! I don't know how you managed to, but you got a drink. I don't think the barman saw me. You were up on a stool. I was down on the ground and all I could do was take out my schoolbooks. I remember looking at my religion book and wanting Jesus to come and get me. You were like somebody else.

JOHN

I know.

MARY

There was a row or something and you fell on top of me.

JOHN

This is awful.

MARY

A ban guard took me home.

JOHN

I know. Terrible things happen. You have a temper and you're not talking to someone. And you calm down and try to keep your heart, fucking, somehow open. But you go and hit the fucking bottle. And you make everything fucking worse. I know you want me to say I'm sorry.

MARY

No . . .

JOHN

(Although calm, he is trawling a black place) But I can hardly remember anything. I was in a very bad state. I don't want to make any excuses, but Jesus Christ! I was in hell. I was in agony. And nobody knew. And I didn't know what to do about it. You don't know. I am sorry. I am sorry. I'm sorry about the whole stinking business. I think about it now and I want to puke. I wish I'd never been born. It's all been awful.

MARY

No. It hasn't all been awful.

JOHN

No. It's been awful for me and I made it terrible for you and your mother and Paul. God. There was one morning I was with Carol, down there in her house, down there in Sybil Hill. And whatever was wrong with me, I was after getting out of bed. I was in bed with this woman, Mary! You were in school. And I went over to the window. She had these venetian blinds with tassels on the end of them. And it was these tassels. I was looking out at her bit of a garden there and these tassels. Tassels on the blinds. And whatever it was, I knew I'd fucking blown it, you know? Because although I'd never would've given a flying shite about blinds and tassels on them it was just something your mother would never have bought. Because it was crummy. It was gaudy or whatever. And I suddenly felt like I was miles and miles away from you and Helen and Pauly. And I knew I couldn't go back. Because I was dirty. I was a dirty filthy dirty man. And you're making me think about it. I'm often wondering where Pauly is. Over in England and all. And if he's thinking about me. God I feel like my brain is going to burst. And you come in and you're so like your mother, and I often, just sometimes wish you'd just fuck off.

MARY

I know.

JOHN

There was this day. I woke up in Carol's house, sick and everything all over my clothes. And I took some of her husband's clothes. She kept them! Oh it was awful. She kept them for all those years. He'd been dead longer than they'd been married. It was like a nightmare. And I put on his gear and started walking home. Hoping to God, for once that your mother would be there! I was changing everything. I needed her to be there. I was going to change it all and get help and basically apologize to everybody. And there I was coming down the road, and I saw her face at the window, looking out, and I was going, "Yes!" "It's all over, I'll never go this low again . . ." And I got in the door and went to where she was there, but it wasn't her, it was the breadboard or something there against the window. So. Do you know what I did?

MARY

I can guess.

JOHN

Yeah, off out on another bender. In a dead man's clothes? "I'll never go this low?" I'd managed to go even further.

(Short pause.)

I knew when it was happening. At the beginning. There was a lot of money knocking about in those days. And a lot of parties. And if I had second sight or something. I knew I was absolutely fucked. Be there in someone's new house at Christmas. People all enjoying themselves, all the fucking wives expecting babies. And it was like I could see the soul of the party or something. The kick off the first few drinks. Like the soul of the party was like a beautiful girl dancing through the room. And then, of course by the end of the night when I'd basically insulted and alienated everyone, the soul of the party was this old fucking cripple that didn't even have the energy to complain or ask for help anymore. Me leaving those places, the fucking silence behind me as I left was ... fucking ... deafening.

MARY

I'm not ... I didn't come here to hurt you.

JOHN

What do you mean?

MARY

I don't know. I feel like I'm hurting you.

JOHN

You can't hurt me. What have I done? *(Short pause. She seems very real to him all of a sudden)* You know? I'm looking at you. I'm looking at you there, you know?

MARY

Do you want me to go? I don't want to go.

JOHN

(He's belting back the whiskey) Oh fucking hell.

MARY

Do you ... ever wish you could ... go back and have it all different?

JOHN

Go back? No way. I just wish it never happened. I don't want anything to exist, you know? Of what happened.

MARY

You don't want me to exist?

JOHN

Not like this! Not with me as your . . . dad.

MARY

(Matter-of-factly, no malice) I'm not happy. (Either.)

JOHN

I know. Don't! This is horrible.

MARY

But I don't know if it's your fault. I'm kind of an eejit as well, on my own, like, you know?

(Pause. They laugh.)

You know?

JOHN

You're an eejit in your own right . . .

MARY

(A little laugh) Yeah.

JOHN

Oh God . . . Well I know where you got it.

MARY

What was Mum like?

(John pours them more drink.)

JOHN

I don't know. I don't know. Quiet. Embarrassed. This is mad. I always felt sorry for her.

MARY

Is that why you were with her?

JOHN

Maybe. I was always sort of fucking perverse. You know?
Doing things for the sheer hell of it. Doing stupid things just
to sort of see what'd happen.

MARY

Were you just pretending. To love her?

JOHN

I don't know. No. Love . . . What the fuck is that, you know.
Ah you just generally get into a sort of a routine. Just . . . Are
you . . . se . . . close?

MARY

Yeah.

(She starts crying.)

Sorry.

(She gets a tissue from her bag, wiping her nose.)

I'm just thinking about her.

(Pause.)

You know, whatever kind of happened to her, because of you
and all that. It, whatever way, she had a great strength or
something, because of it.

JOHN

Okay.

MARY

There was humor, even, you know?

JOHN

Yeah.

MARY

I'm talking about her in the past already.

JOHN

Well that's . . . you know, you want to get it over with.

MARY

I know I love her, you know?

JOHN

You're full of fucking loving everybody today and all that.
Yeah?

MARY

(Gently) You're horrible. Were you always this horrible?

JOHN

I don't mean it.

MARY

She was very lenient and all, you know? On Paul. God, he
was a handful. The guards were looking for him and everything, you know?

JOHN

For what?

MARY

Ah he told some ban guard to go fuck herself. In town somewhere.

JOHN

What happened?

MARY

Ah I don't know. She told him to be quiet coming out of a
pub or something.

JOHN

Is he a fucking eeejit, is he?

MARY

No! He's great. But I remember Mum sitting at the kitchen table laughing. And lighting up a fag. And I remember thinking about her. Right then. And knowing that I loved her. Right in that moment. That's how I know. And I was thinking about you. And I was thinking that you'd be really good friends. And it was sort of a pity or something that you were a man and a woman, you know. Like if you could have both been men, or both been women. I don't know. I just remember that, you know?

JOHN

Or if we were just bloody older. You know? Or maybe being older doesn't even make any difference. You just have to be good, don't you? That's the thing. The man who owns this business was very good to me. I've never been good to any-body. There's something I can't help it. I needed like a teacher or something. The man who runs this business, Noel, he's in hospital having tests done, right? And he's such a kind and a, a, a good person. He doesn't deserve to be sick, nobody does, you know? But there I was, visiting him there. And do you know what was going through my mind? I was going, part of me was, it was like a little tune, I didn't know what it was until I listened to it. I was thinking, Here you are all tucked up in hospital, all fucking not well and all this. And I'm up and about, bullshitting for Ireland, rapping along with barmen, and you never hurt a fly. But you're a stupid cunt, because you're sick. You're a wanker, because you're all weak and sick there, taking your medicine. I felt like I hated him because the poor bastard isn't well. You see, that's mean. That's what I have.

MARY

I don't think that matters. I . . . I don't care.

JOHN

Well I blow my own fucking mind.

MARY

You were sick too. You were sick in your head.

JOHN

I was just sick of my fucking self.

MARY

But that's . . . that's the same.

JOHN

(Slightly dismissive) Yeah, yeah.

MARY

(Wanting to prove that she is like him) Everybody hated me.

JOHN

What do you mean?

MARY

I was a weird girl.

JOHN

No you weren't.

MARY

When I got older. You'd see me walking around the estate on my own, walking the dog and having a smoke.

JOHN

What dog?

MARY

We got a dog. Snoopy.

JOHN

Really? It's like I feel like I have a dog now.

MARY

He's dead.

JOHN

Okay.

MARY

People used to say that girl's not right.

JOHN

People are only stupid. Ganging up on you.

MARY

I didn't care. I liked it. It made me feel like I was closer to you because I was sort of like you.

JOHN

(Shakes his head slowly) Em.

MARY

(Reading him) But I was only playing at it.

JOHN

You didn't destroy your life. But someone saved me. You know?

MARY

I think that's what I was looking for.

JOHN

You don't need it.

(Pause.)

MARY

What happened to you?

(Pause.)

JOHN

Boredom. Loneliness. A feeling of basically being out of step with everybody else. Fear. Anxiety. Tension. And of course, a disposition to generally liking the whole fucking thing of drinking until you pass out.

MARY

But what were you worried about?

(Pause.)

JOHN

I just always felt like people were judging me. I just always felt guilty.

MARY

Why?

JOHN

I don't know. Why do all these young . . . drug addicts . . . I see people my generation. You see them there in their suit jackets. Sitting on some street corner. Begging for money for drink. You think they don't know it's a short-term solution? They know. But the long-term is terrifying. Failure reaching up and grabbing you. We were brought up like that a little bit. You know? That we were all going to hell or somewhere. You know?

(Short pause.)

My dad used to beat the living daylights out of my mother, you know? *(Pause)* He used used to come in and hammer the fucking head off her. Tusssss. And you're only a young boy. You're fucking hiding under the bed, you'd hear him come in roaring. And . . . It wasn't that I was going, "I'm too young to do anything." It was something else. I was just . . . shit scared. And I let her take it. So he wouldn't hit me. That feeling went away, when I got older. He became a little frail old man and stopped all that shenanigans. And I fucking just generally forgot about it, you know? But then, years later, when you were born, right? I started to feel again like I was a ... coward. Do you see I thought the world was a bad place and that someone was going to come and attack us.

MARY

Who?

JOHN

I don't know. But somewhere in me. I knew ... I'd let you ... and your mammy ... down. That if we were attacked. I knew deep down in me, that I'd run away and leave yous to it. You a little baby. And your mother like a little squirrel or something.

MARY

No one was going to attack us.

JOHN

I knew that! But this was a thing that I couldn't help feeling. And it was a terrible fucking feeling to have. And I just believed in it. And I sort of, let yous all down, just to get it over with. Or something.

(Pause.)

I don't understand it.

(Pause.)

MARY

You could do her funeral.

JOHN

Oh No! No! Mary, no!

MARY

Is that ...

JOHN

Aw God, Jesus, no ...

MARY

That's . . . yeah?

JOHN

I couldn't.

MARY

I know.

JOHN

Bad enough, seeing her, but putting her down, in the muck, for fuck's sake Mary.

MARY

Okay.

JOHN

Yeah. There in her dressing gown?! A man in his pajamas is bad enough. But a woman there in her nightdress. Very much a lady and not a man. And the betrayal and the guilt and everything written all over our fucking faces.

MARY

Don't drink anymore.

JOHN

What?

MARY

Don't drink anymore before you see her. Be sober, alright?

JOHN

I am sober.

MARY

Yeah but don't drink anymore. *(She becomes upset)* Please.

JOHN

(Aggravated) Okay. Alright. Jesus.

MARY

I'm sorry.

JOHN

No. Oh God!

MARY

Don't see her if . . . you can't.

JOHN

(Inhales deeply) Oh Mary.

MARY

I'll say I couldn't see you or . . .

(John puts his hand to his face.)

Okay? *(Short pause)* I'll tell her I couldn't find you.

JOHN

(Exhales) No.

MARY

I'll help you. We'll go together.

(She wants to go near him. But stays where she is.)

Dad.

(John looks at her.)

I'll help you. I'll be with you.

JOHN

(Accepting) Yeah. *(Beat)* Yeah.

(There's a long pause. In which neither knows what to say.)

MARY

I'll call here at five.

JOHN

Okay.

MARY

(As much to convince herself as him) It'll be alright. It'll be alright.

JOHN

I . . . want to make it up to you.

MARY

Nnn . . . *(Unable to take anymore)* I'm gonna call back at five. Okay, Dad?

JOHN

I'll be here.

(She stays for a moment. And then leaves. John stands there. The lights fade.)

PART THREE

✛

We hear the bells chiming. Four o'clock. John is slumped in a chair. Three quarters of the whiskey is gone. He sleeps in a drunken stupor. There is a soft knocking at the door.

MARK

(Off) Mr. Plunkett?

(Mark opens the door and steps in. He is in casual gear now, and consequently looks younger.)

Mr. Plunkett?

(John is startled.)

JOHN

What? Paul?

MARK

It's Mark.

JOHN

What are you doing? I haven't gone to the bank.

MARK

Oh. Okay.

JOHN

What time is it?

MARK

Are you alright?

JOHN

Have I missed the bank? What time is it?

MARK

It's five past four.

JOHN

Bollocks. Ah for fuck's sake. I'm sorry.

(John fishes into his pockets.)

Are you waiting on it? How much are you owed?

MARK

Forget about it.

JOHN

Ah for fuck's sake, I'm sorry. Here. What's this?

(John counts some money out of his pocket. It's all different notes bundled in little balls.)

I'm just, I'm sorry, I've had a horrible . . . What's this? Look there's thirty . . . five . . . Ah I'm sorry.

MARK

Ah it's okay.

JOHN

Will that do you?

MARK

Ah yeah, no, that's grand.

JOHN

I have to go.

(John tries to get his coat. He knocks some furniture over, Mark helps him.)

MARK

Are you okay?

JOHN

I need the toilet.

(Mark gets him to the toilet.)

Will you put the kettle on?

MARK

Yeah. Sure.

(John goes into the toilet. Mark puts water in the kettle and turns it on. He then stands there, leaning, lost in thought.

John reappears, wiping his mouth with some tissue. He watches Mark. Mark doesn't notice him.)

JOHN

Are you alright?

MARK

(Snapping out of it) Yeah. Are you okay?

JOHN

Yeah, I just. I had a good bit to drink. *(Realizing Mark's demeanor)* Have you had a few?

MARK

I've had a couple.

(John watches Mark making the tea.)

JOHN

You're not very full of Christmas cheer.

(Mark acknowledges this. A snort.)

Do you want a drink?

MARK

Is that alright?

JOHN

Of course it is! Christmas Eve!

MARK

Thanks.

(Mark pours himself a drink.)

Do you want one?

JOHN

Oh Jesus, just give me a small one. Just put a drop in my tea.

(Mark pours a drink for John and hands it to him.)

Thanks.

(Mark takes a large slug of whiskey. He doesn't seem used to it.)

Are you alright?

MARK

Yeah.

JOHN

Do you want to maybe put some water in that?

MARK

No, it's okay.

(Mark takes another large slug.)

JOHN

Are you annoyed with me or something?

MARK

What?

JOHN

Are you annoyed at me about your money?

MARK

Ah, no. No.

JOHN

What's wrong with you?

MARK

Nothing. I just didn't have a . . . brilliant afternoon. I'm fine.

JOHN

What happened?

MARK

Nothing.

(Pause.)

JOHN

Okay.

MARK

Just. When I left here I was going to do something. And I didn't do it, you know?

JOHN

What is it? Do you want me to do it for you?

MARK

(A little laugh) No. Eh . . . you know Kim. I was telling you . . . earlier.

JOHN

Don't tell me you didn't get her something.

MARK

No. No, no, no.

(Pause.)

JOHN

What's wrong?

MARK

I just went down to break it off with her, you know?

JOHN

On . . . Christmas Eve?

MARK

No. It's just, she's all on for us to go away together next week. You know? And I don't want to just be making excuses. So I . . . I know it's not a great time. But you know, she's become . . . very intense. About me. And I'm not . . . you know the same.

JOHN

You're not the same about her.

MARK

No.

JOHN

Tch. So you toddled off to tell her.

(Mark nods.)

Down in Marino.

MARK

Yeah.

(Pause.)

She'd been in work. She started at six or four this morning or something. She was knackered. And I went in to tell her. To her gaff. Her ma let me go up. She was having a lie down.

JOHN

(Gives a little laugh) This is not brilliant.

MARK

I know.

JOHN

What did you say?

(Pause.)

MARK

Mr. Plunkett. *(Beat)* I don't know. I just was blurting away there. Just her face . . . Just this really faint high-pitched noise started to come out of her.

JOHN

It just couldn't have gone worse. I know. Don't worry about it.

MARK

No . . .

JOHN

She probably has some serious mental disability or something.

MARK

She started sort of grabbing me. And this . . . noise. I was, here, it's okay, it's okay.

(John snorts.)

I thought that like if she was my sister or something. I just stayed there with her. Like no one should . . . (Cause this much hurt.) I basically told her I didn't mean it. I've been on my own in the pub across the road for two hours.

(Mark looks at John.)

JOHN

Mmm. Well, you know, it might look like you made a bollocks of it.

MARK

Well that's what it feels like.

JOHN

Yeah, but she might've been pulling a sneaky on you, you know?

MARK

No this was, this was real, man.

JOHN

Here, give us a drop of that. Give yourself a lash. *(Looks around sharply)* What time is it?

(Mark pours them both some whiskey.)

Okay, it was real. She had a genuine freak attack, but there's an element of blackmail, in that, do you know what I mean?

(Pause.)

MARK

That she did it on purpose?

JOHN

She mightn't have done it completely on purpose, but when she felt it coming on, you know? She let the fucking thing fly. You know?

(Mark laughs.)

I'm telling you. You wouldn't be up to them.

MARK

Ah I don't think she'd . . . you know?

JOHN

Yeah but look at it now. Here's you all fretting. You're getting all limbered up to go on a fucking bender. All fucking despair and moaning to your mates on Christmas Eve, all tomorrow wondering if she's gonna eat a bottle of tablets, or end up in Grangegorman, you know? And where's she? She's tucked up in bed, with her mammy filling her full of cup-a-soup and talking about watching *Raiders of the Lost Ark* later on and pulling the couch over to the fire and eating chocolate liquers. Do you see what I mean?

MARK

(Laughs) I just don't think it was on purpose.

JOHN

Look you had a difficult thing to do. You were going down there to tell her the truth. And it was gonna be hard, because I can see by you that you're a sensitive kind of chap, and you were concerned about her feelings. You aren't in the business of dishing out pain and agony and not giving a bollocks. So there you are trying to give the whole thing a bit of respect. It's not like you were doing a bunk with some black girl or hopping on the next train to Timbuktu. You did the hard thing. And what does she do?

MARK

She might have been still kind of asleep or something though.

JOHN

Yeah but you're upset as well, but you're engaging in it in a grown-up way of sitting down and talking about it. We can all throw fits. We can all lose the head. But that's selfish, though, as well. Because it's mean. It's, "Fuck you. I'm not talking to you." No acknowledgment that you're trying to do the right thing or nothing, none of that. Just basically, "Ah

75

you've driven me into the grave, and now you're cursed by the gypsies of County Carlow," you know? It's bollocks.

(Pause.)

MARK

I should ring her.

JOHN

Nah! Let her ring you. She's probably fucking stalking you now, anyway. She's probably across the road with a pitchfork.

(Mark gives a little laugh.)

Anyway. That's dangerous love. It's different kinds of love that men and women give. A woman's love can be terribly constant. Good God. It can last for years! *(Pause)* There was this woman loved me unconditionally for many years. Gave me lifts everywhere. Waited for me. And waited for me in the long term as well. Waiting on me . . . She was a widow, you know? And I was still married. I was going into a nose dive on the booze. It had a real hold of me. She was very very lonely. Living in a house up there in Sybil Hill. She was holding down this part-time job. Not much money. She had a little Fiat 127.

She used to drink pots of tea up there in The Beachcomber in Killester up there. And I'd be skiving off work early, sneaking around pubs all up in Raheny and Killester and Harmonstown and then all down here and into town.

Got chatting to her in The Beachcomber. And she hooked me because she could see that I was very taken with getting bollocksed and she'd buy me drinks. And it got that I'd . . . I'd rely on her being in there. This is mad, you know? And then it was whiskey up in the gaff. *(Pause)* And I followed the trail of breadcrumbs all the way into bed. I was more into the drink than the sex though. She was into neither. She just couldn't take it on her own. Being on her own. So there we were. Her loving me and me treating it like a convenience.

I thought of it like God had sent me like a drink-angel. Like I believed in God and he'd sent this to take care of me. And that she was like all confused because she didn't know why God had sent her. And she didn't know why she loved me but she just did. God I used to feel sorry for her. Giving me her last bit of money. Giving me her last fiver and me asking her if she didn't have anymore?! Counting out her change trying to get it up to the four pints! But that was the awful disservice I was doing her. The vanity. No it wasn't vanity. Just that I'd been taught to believe in God! Poor stupid bitch. You have no idea. You have no idea.

But that was it. I had somewhere to go where I'd get bollocksed and blot out that I had a, a, a fucking life somewhere else. So it was easy. And that's dangerous love. That unconditional, "I'll do anything to keep you," fucking thing. God she had me pickled. You're well shot of this one and that's the end of it. What are you going to do? Basically torture yourself until you feel better? You won't feel better so just . . . bollocks.

(Pause.)

MARK

Mmm.

JOHN

Yeah.

(Mark pours himself a nip of whiskey and pours some into John's mug.)

MARK

But that's like a fit as well.

77

JOHN

What?

MARK

You baling off, on your family.

JOHN

(Considers) I'm in a fog.

MARK

Like, you're saying about Kim, that she threw a freaker and that's . . . not fair on me.

JOHN

(Vaguely affirmative) Uhh.

MARK

You doing a bunk. How is that . . . facing . . . up . . .

JOHN

Well, that's how I know what I'm talking about.

MARK

That's bollocks.

JOHN

What am I supposed to do? Stand here and defend myself all day?

MARK

Well then don't be dispensing fucking . . . wisdom . . . I feel like a fucking asshole! You're here telling me what to do? *(Fiercely)* I just feel like a fucking eejit!

JOHN

I'm only trying to help you! Why don't you let me finish?! I'm like the opposite of you . . . What? Am I talking to you like you're a kid? Is that it?

(Pause.)

What do you want?

MARK

I'm, look . . . I'll see you later.

(Mark starts to go.)

JOHN

Don't go like this, Mark. It's Christmas.

MARK

Fuck off.

(Mark is leaving.)

JOHN

My wife is dying. I need someone I can talk to, son.

MARK

What?

JOHN

She has cancer in her neck.

(Pause.)

MARK

This is your wife?

JOHN

Yeah. I haven't seen her for eh, for many years now, you know?

MARK

I'm sorry . . . to hear that.

JOHN

Yeah, well. You know, it's not something I should eh, I should be sympathized with about really. You know?

(Silence.)

They want me to do her funeral.

(Long pause.)

What do you think?

MARK

I . . . don't know . . .

JOHN

You're right, you know? About me.

MARK

Look. I don't . . .

JOHN

(Slightly too bossy) Listen to me! *(Apologetic)* I'm sorry. No. Listen. Listen to me. I'm sorry.

MARK

It's okay. It's alright.

JOHN

My daughter's coming. I don't have much time. She wants me to go to the hospital and see her. I'm just, I really don't know what to do. Your Uncle Noel would know.

(Short pause.)

MARK

You should go.

JOHN

Yeah?

MARK

You . . . probably should. What if you don't . . . And she . . .

(Pause.)

JOHN

No. No, you're right. *(Pause. Facing a terrible prospect)* Paul, he's my . . . son, you know? He's coming home from England. And I haven't seen him since he was eh . . . *(Pause)* He came around here one time a few years ago. Looking for me. *(Screws up his face a little)* And I said I wasn't here, you know? They told him I wasn't here. And I just sat over there, waiting until he was gone. And then I changed my mind and went out after him. I just kept going up and down the North Strand looking for him. But, he was gone obviously and that was all there was about it. But I got a letter from him a bit later, telling me he got his Leaving Cert. This is a few years ago. Yeah. What time is it?

MARK

Half four.

JOHN

I better drink some tea.

(John begins to get up.)

MARK

I'll get it.

(John sniffs.)

JOHN

Thanks. Here, you might as well do the Advent calendar. We won't be here tomorrow.

(Mark gives a little laugh.)

MARK

Okay.

JOHN

Have a little thrill. Knock yourself out.

(Mark laughs. He opens the last door on the Advent calendar.)

What is it?

MARK

It's Jesus.

JOHN

Of course it is. Will you do something for me?

MARK

Yeah.

JOHN

There should be an old box out there in the yard. I want to get the decorations down.

(Mark goes to the door and comes back with a box.)

MARK

I'll give you a hand.

(Mark begins taking things down.)

JOHN

There's nothing worse than decorations after Christmas. That's the way I sometimes used to feel putting my clothes on in the morning.

(John helps Mark.)

And that special alcoholic's hangover. I pray you never get one. It's a fucking beaut. It's after a couple of days on the serious piss. What happens is, day one, for whatever reason, you've started early and basically polluted yourself. It's a form of poisoning. And so, on day two, you are in the absolute horrors. I don't mean what most people feel like after their Christmas party, sick tummy and a headache. This is a raging dose of the screaming paranoid shits. You're shit scared. Just to walk down the street you think you're going to be beaten up. And there's a sickening disgust with yourself to boot, and there's only one thing you can do to stop it.

MARK

More drink.

JOHN

Bingo. On day two, you can get shit-faced very easily, because of all the alcohol your poor demented liver still hasn't had time to process, and neutralized. Technically you're still drunk. Oh but it's a bad drunk. So you'll feel okay after a few scoops, normal in fact, and ironically, not very drunk. You don't feel drunk. You feel normal. And you say to yourself, "How brilliant it'd be to feel normal like this all the time and not need to get the booze into you at a horrifying rate." But you know this feeling is going to go away, so you bale into a few more drinks. And then you begin to feel drunk. Drunk drunk. A bit euphoric and a bit fearless and generally a bit numb to all the bad feelings and the worries. But all the time there's the little niggle that it's going to disappear, so you won't even eat in case you might dilute the effect. And before you know it, you've passed out for two days in a row. Day three is a weird one. Well it always was for me. You've got the screaming paranoid shits back but your poor body is saying, "No more. I can't take it." You'll puke if you tear into it. So you have to be a bit crafty and . . . sneak up on yourself. Lie on. Sleep it off a bit. Maybe eat a bit of a fry in the Kylemore or Bewley's or somewhere. And then, slowly, leisurely and generally a bit fucking nonchalantly have a few decent pints in a hotel bar or somewhere nice. Where you're not surrounded by a bunch of fucking mungos. And you'll be very tired but you won't be able to sleep. You'll just drowse enough to have a few terrifying dreams and wake up crying and all that. Day four you won't be so bad. But it won't be long before day one rolls around again.

(Short pause.)

MARK

That sounds fucking awful!

JOHN

Yeah. Well. That's what Carol, the widow, that's what she was funding for me. She didn't know. She just wanted me to be happy. But massive highs and massive lows is not happy. Not in anybody's books. No. Noel has me sussed. I'm a mouth and a show off. He's calm. And not, just basically not a cunt about it. We'll go for a drink in the evenings. Granted, I'll drink twice as much as him. Say six pints to his two or three. But then it's into bed at a reasonable hour and you'll have had your tea and all that. So it's a stark contrast to the boys with the big sunburnt heads, having a belt off a bottle of meths before generally just sort of doing your toilet straight into your trousers.

(John seriously regards Mark for a moment.)

Don't be worrying. Okay?

MARK

Yeah, I'm . . .

JOHN

I know. You just take it nice and handy now. I think you're probably a born worrier, are you?

MARK

I think I might be.

JOHN

Yeah. Do you know what would be brilliant? For you?

MARK

Yeah?

JOHN

Just to be incredibly fucking thick. Do you know what I mean?

(They laugh.)

You know?

MARK

Yeah.

JOHN

Yeah . . .

MARK

You're not going to be on your own, are you? Tomorrow?

JOHN

I don't know. I suppose I was going to be. With Noel out of action. I was gonna go in and see him, you know?

MARK

We're going in in the morning. Me and Mum.

JOHN

Ah yeah. Good. Yeah I was gonna do that and then, I don't know. Watch the telly. But. I don't know. To tell you the truth, I'm not gonna get worked up about it. Tomorrow is Saturday and that's all. Another filthy morning, only there's a star in the East. Yeah. Is that it?

MARK

Nearly. The Advent calendar.

JOHN

Oh yeah.

(John goes and takes the Advent calendar down from the wall.)

They should have one of these with all year on it.

MARK

Yeah.

JOHN

With little words of wisdom. Little cautionary words of advice. The second of July. A word of caution. Fourth of August, a word to the wise. You know? November, "You're being a spa, cop on to yourself, you know?"

MARK

A few jokes.

JOHN

A few jokes. Now you're talking. Mister Doom and Gloom over here. Are you going into town?

MARK

Yeah.

JOHN

You've enough money.

MARK

Yeah, I'm fine. Not gonna be too late anyway.

JOHN

Get into bed before Santa comes and checks.

MARK

And leaves me a bag of soot.

JOHN

Or slips Kim in your stocking.

MARK

(A slightly sad laugh) Oh fuck.

JOHN

The imagination's gone fucko now.

(Mark puts on his coat. He takes out a Walkman and untangles the headphones.)

Oh Walkman! Noel gave me one a few Christmases ago. For sitting outside the church. You couldn't put the radio on in the hearse. It'd be awful, obviously. But you can slip in a little earphone, get the news and that. Yeah, great.

MARK

Yeah.

JOHN

A woman singing in your ear, ha?

(Mark gives a little amused snort. He turns the tape in the machine over.)

Do you have a radio on that?

MARK

Oh yeah. I think there's nearly radios on all of them now.

JOHN

You know if you're listening to the radio and there's all static and you put your hand on it.

MARK

Yeah, you earth it.

JOHN

Yeah and there's a clear signal. It'd be great to be able to do that, wouldn't it? To people, I mean. To people.

(Short pause.)

MARK

Yeah.

JOHN

Go on. I'm losing the plot. Get outta here. Get out among the living.

MARK

I'll see you on Monday.

JOHN

Yeah there's some poor bastard out there. Looking forward to the old Xmas, not knowing he'll be under this roof on Monday waiting to be buried.

MARK

(A little laugh) Could be you or me.

JOHN

Nah . . . *(Gives a little laugh)* Go on, have a good time.

MARK

Okay.

(They shake hands.)

Happy Christmas. I'm sorry . . . for your wife.

JOHN

Yeah, Happy Christmas. Thanks. Don't eat too much cake.

MARK

Alright. I'll see you.

(Mark goes.)

JOHN

(Calling after him) And don't be worrying, do you hear me?

MARK

(Off) Yeah, I know.

(John nods. We hear the outer door slam shut.

John stands there for a moment and then looks around. He goes and takes a towel from a press and goes to the sink. He pauses and switches on a little transistor radio. Festive music is playing. He takes some soap and washes his face and neck and dries himself briskly.

He fixes his tie carefully and puts on his jacket and overcoat. Then he takes a comb and does his hair in a little mirror. He is ready. He stands there collecting himself.

He looks at the box of decorations. He considers them. He goes to the box and takes out the Advent calendar. He holds it for a moment and decisively places it back on the wall where it was. He returns to the box. He overturns it on the table. He selects some stuff and begins to put the decorations back up. He stands on a chair, redecorating. From nearby the church bells chime out five o'clock.

The lights begin to fade, then the music and the bells.)

E N D   O F   P L A Y

CONOR MCPHERSON was born in 1971 in Dublin, where he still resides. He graduated from University College Dublin (UCD) in 1993 with an MA degree in philosophy, and later worked for two years in UCD's Philosophy Department as a tutor in Ethics and Moral Philosophy.

His plays include *This Lime Tree Bower, St. Nicholas, The Good Thief, Rum and Vodka* and *The Weir* (winner of the 1999 Olivier Award for Best Play), all of which have been published by TCG in *The Weir and Other Plays*. He is the recipient of numerous awards for playwriting, including the *Evening Standard* Award for Outstanding New Playwright and the London Critics' Circle Award for Most Promising Playwright. He is co-founder of the Fly By Night Theatre Company, which performed new plays in Dublin's fringe venues. In 1996 he was appointed writer-in-residence at London's Bush Theatre.

Mr. McPherson's film work includes *I Went Down*, for which he wrote the screenplay, and which won Best New Screenplay at the San Sebastian Film Festival. He recently directed *Saltwater* (his adaptation of *This Lime Tree Bower*), which won the CICAE Award for Best Film at the Berlin Film Festival. He has just completed directing a film adaptation of Beckett's *Endgame*, and in spring 2001 will begin writing and directing a feature film for Neil Jordan and DreamWorks Productions.